W9-CHN-177

The KnowHow Book of
Paper Fun

Written and devised by:
Annabelle Curtis and Judy Hindley

Illustrated by Colin King

Designed by John Jamieson

With the help of Penelope Ford,
age 12, Miranda Ford, age 8, and
Anna Hindley, age 8

Educational Adviser Frank Blackwell

First published in 1975
Usborne Publishing Ltd
20 Garrick Street
London WC 2

© Usborne Publishing Ltd 1975

Printed in Great Britain by
Purnell & Sons Ltd
Bristol

About This Book

This is a book about all kinds of things to do and make with paper, from tricks with newspaper to paper flowers and paper sculpture. There are lots of big projects and some quick ones to do as soon as you take the book home. The projects at the beginning are easier to make than those at the end of the book.

For many of the projects all you need are paper, scissors, ruler and glue. Remember that the right kind of glue is important – use Bostik 1 or UHU. Page 46 tells you where to find special materials.

Boxes with this sign give you special tips for making the projects work.

The KnowHow Book of Paper Fun

Contents

Paper Tricks

1 Magic Ladder

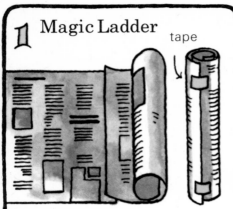

tape

Lay out two sheets of newspaper, like this, and roll them up. Fasten the ends with sticky tape.

2

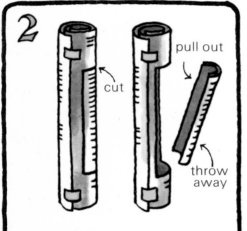

cut

pull out

throw away

Cut out the piece shown here. Throw this piece away.

3

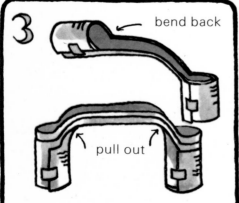

bend back

pull out

Bend the roll back to make a bridge shape. Gently pull out the insides from each side. Here comes the ladder!

The more sheets of paper you use, the higher your ladder will go. Paper ladders can go as high as a two-storey house! (But you need strong hands to cut or tear through so much newspaper.)

Surprise Tricks

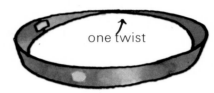

one twist

Twist a strip of paper and tape it into a loop. Put a red spot on the paper. Run your finger round and round the loop. Which is the inside of the loop?

cut

two twists

Now make a loop with two twists. Cut as shown to make two loops. Surprised?

Q: If you got lost in a blizzard with the Sunday papers, what would you do?

A: Cover your head and stuff your clothes with newspaper. Layers of newspaper trap thin sandwiches of air warmed by your body. (This is a real survival trick.)

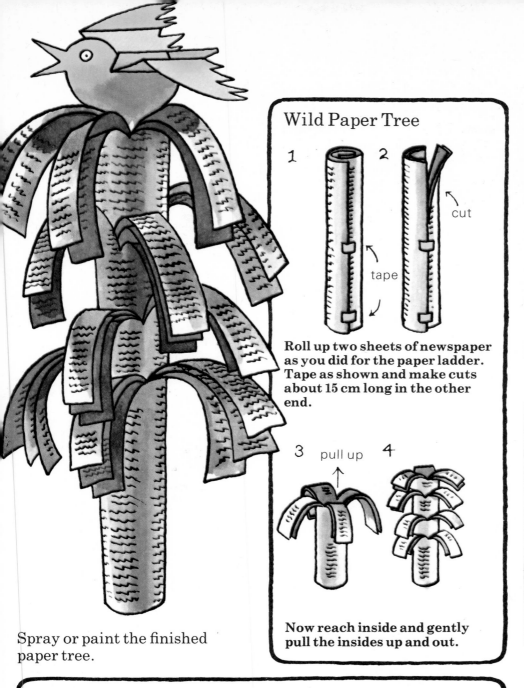

Spray or paint the finished paper tree.

Wild Paper Tree

1 **2**

tape *cut*

Roll up two sheets of newspaper as you did for the paper ladder. Tape as shown and make cuts about 15 cm long in the other end.

3 *pull up* **4**

Now reach inside and gently pull the insides up and out.

1 Sitting Bird

same size

Draw a long-legged bird on stiff paper and cut it out. Fold some paper and make a wing to fit the bird's back.

2

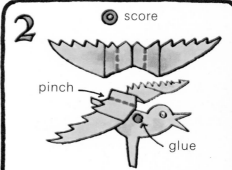

● score

pinch

glue

Unfold the wing and score as shown. Fold each side towards the centre. Put glue on each side of the back, pinch on the wing and poke the leg into the top of the tree.

Walk Through a Postcard

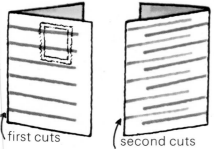

first cuts *second cuts*

unfold

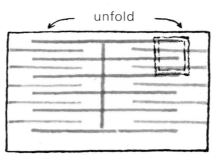

Fold the card. Make cuts from the fold almost to the edges. Now make another set of cuts from the edges almost to the fold. Don't cut through!

Open the card out and cut along the fold. But don't cut through the outside edges! Tug and see what happens.

◎ How to Score

To score a straight line run the tip of your scissors along the paper against a ruler. Score curved lines without a ruler. Fold the paper firmly.

Crazy Tops and Whirlers

You will need
some card
a cup to draw the circle
paints or crayons
string and scissors
small round sticks or pencil ends

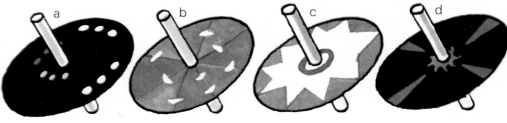

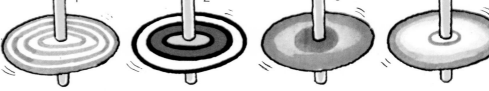

Q: Match the top row with the spinners (answer below).

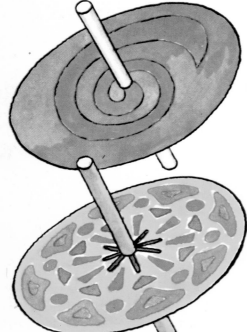

Can you do the puzzle at the top of the page? Moving things make patterns that can fool your eyes. Try these special patterns and see what happens.

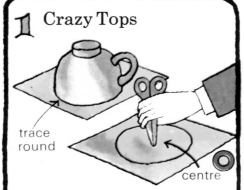

1 Crazy Tops

Draw and cut out a circle of card. Make a small hole in the centre. Always point sharp things away from you.

trace round

centre

2

glue

same length

glue

Glue the circle right at the middle of the stick. Remember – your circles must fit tightly at the middle.

Find the Centre of a Circle

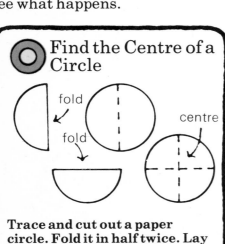

fold

fold

centre

Trace and cut out a paper circle. Fold it in half twice. Lay this pattern on the card and make a hole where the two folds cross.

Whirlers

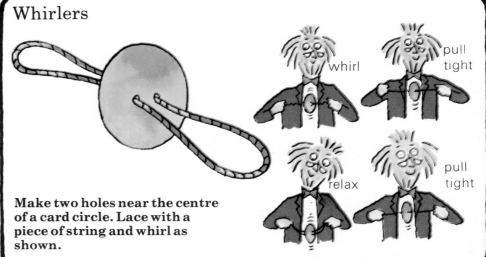

whirl

pull tight

relax

pull tight

Make two holes near the centre of a card circle. Lace with a piece of string and whirl as shown.

A: a–2, b–1, c–4, d–3

Jumping Spiders and Butterflies

You will need
a small box
acetate (see-through plastic,
  often used for boxes of cards)
scissors and sticky tape
stiff paper and tissue paper

Just rub the
acetate and
watch them
creep and flutter

1 Spiders and Butterflies

bend down

twist

**Spiders – cut from stiff paper.
Bend the legs as shown.**

**Butterflies – cut from tissue
paper. Twist in the middle or
they won't keep moving.**

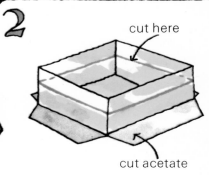

2

cut here

cut acetate

**Cut down a small box, like this.
Cut some acetate to fit over
the box.**

Static Electricity

**When you rub certain things
you get static electricity. This
is why your butterflies and
spiders jump. Static electricity
makes your hair stick out when
you comb it hard on a very dry,
cold day. In a dark room you
might see sparks! Try it the
next time you find that you
have frizzy hair.**

3

cover with acetate

tape down

**Fill the box with six or seven
butterflies or spiders. Tape
acetate over the box.**

Pop-Up Cards

You will need
scissors and ruler
paints or crayons
pencil and glue
stiff paper

Fold carefully and crease hard
to make a pop-up card that really
pops. If you use very stiff paper,
it is a good idea to score the folds.
Remember – How to Score, p.5.

1 Ghost Pop-Up
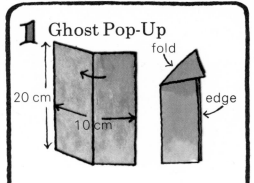

20 cm
10 cm
fold
edge

Use a piece of paper twice as
long as it is wide. Fold in half
as shown. Then fold the top
corner from the centre fold to
the edge. Crease by folding
back and forth.

2
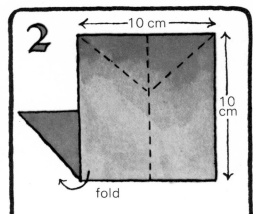

10 cm
10 cm
fold

Open the card. Now fold
the bottom edge to the top
as shown.

3
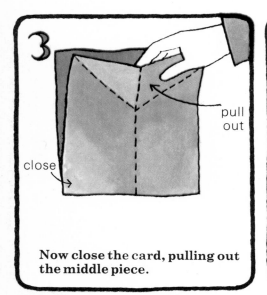

pull
out

close

Now close the card, pulling out
the middle piece.

4
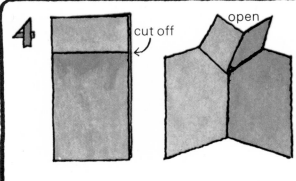
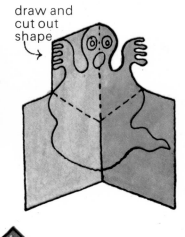

cut off
open
draw and
cut out
shape

Cut off the top edge of the card.
When you open it again the
inside will pop up. Cut out and
decorate the pop-up.

◎ How to Mark a Straight Line
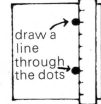
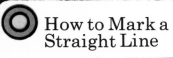

measure and
dot

draw a
line
through
the dots

To cut paper the right size,
measure from the edge and
make a dot at the right number
of centimetres. Do this twice.
Draw a line through the dots
and cut this line.

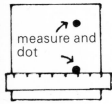

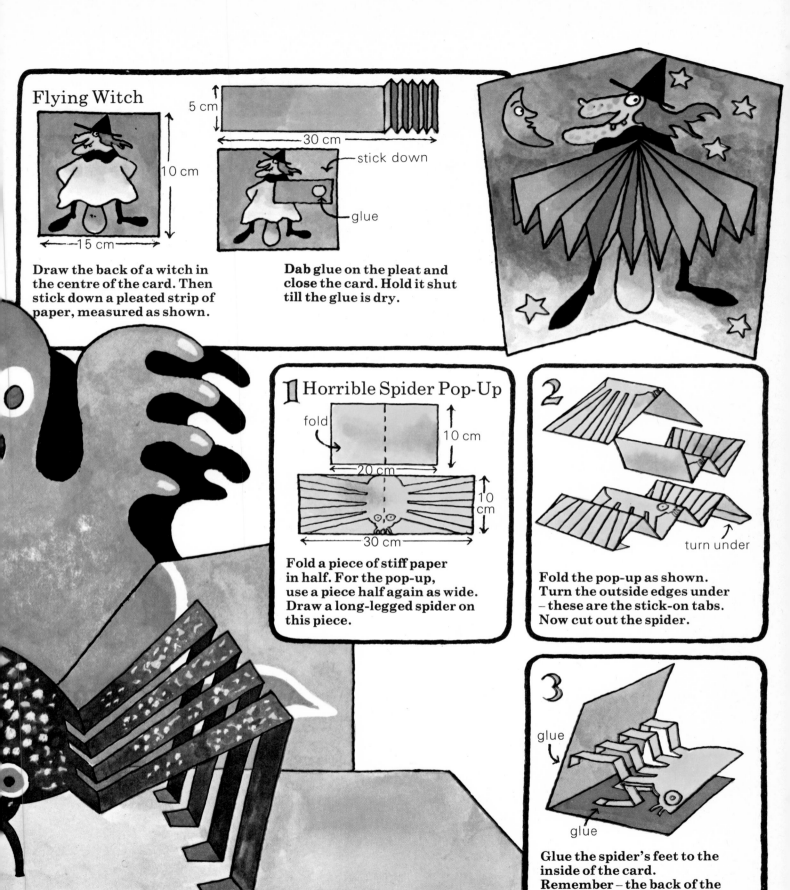

Flying Witch

5 cm
30 cm

← stick down
← glue

10 cm
←15 cm→

Draw the back of a witch in the centre of the card. Then stick down a pleated strip of paper, measured as shown.

Dab glue on the pleat and close the card. Hold it shut till the glue is dry.

1 Horrible Spider Pop-Up

fold →
10 cm
20 cm
10 cm
30 cm

Fold a piece of stiff paper in half. For the pop-up, use a piece half again as wide. Draw a long-legged spider on this piece.

2

turn under

Fold the pop-up as shown. Turn the outside edges under – these are the stick-on tabs. Now cut out the spider.

3

glue →
glue

Glue the spider's feet to the inside of the card. Remember – the back of the folded spider must not stick out over the card edge.

Shadow Cut-Outs

You will need
stiff paper and sticky tape
scissors and pencil
coloured cellophane (from sweet
    wrappers)
torch or lamp

There have been a few great
scissor-artists who could cut
very detailed pictures without
drawing. One trick they used
was to stick black cut-outs on
coloured or painted paper,
which is a good way to decorate
cards or book-covers. With
folded cut-outs you can make
quick paper scenes.

Shadow Machine

Before the camera was
invented, many people paid
artists to make pictures of
their shadows. They would
keep these, or give them to
their friends, like snapshots.
To have their shadow pictures
taken, people sat in chairs
like this one. The artist drew
round the shadow cast on
the screen.

Street at Night

cut

do not cut

**Fold a long strip of paper
back and forth, matching
the folds. Cut out as shown.**

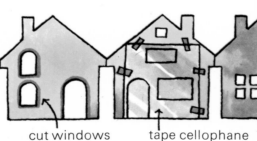
cut windows   tape cellophane

**Unfold. Cut out the windows.
Tape coloured cellophane to
the back of them so that
coloured light comes through.**

Stand-Up Scenery

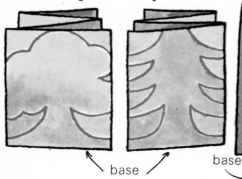
base

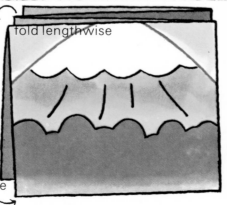
fold lengthwise
base

**Build up 3-D scenes with
several cut-outs. Use the
straight edge of the paper**

**as the base. If the paper is
thin, fold lengthwise first.
Leave some of the top uncut.**

Shadow Pictures

At a party, make shadow pictures of the guests. Tape some paper to the wall and have one of the guests sit close. Darken the room. Place a lamp near his head to cast a crisp shadow. Trace the shadow and cut it out.

trace shadow

Glue the cut-out to a circle of white paper and then to a folded piece of stiff coloured paper.

Stand-Up Animals

cut

bend

Here are two animal patterns that make a stand-up row. Fold as before and cut out. Don't cut through the fold

completely. Bend as shown and the row will stand up by itself.

Stand-Up Fence

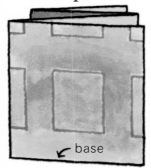

bend

base

Fold paper back and forth and cut as shown. Bend to make it stand up.

How to Cut

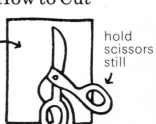

turn paper back and forth

hold scissors still

Remember – always turn the paper, not the scissors. Hold your scissors-hand still and turn the paper with your other hand.

Haunted House Peep-Show

Because of the way your eye works, paper figures can look mysteriously large and real when you squint at them through a peep-hole. Attach some of the figures to threads and pull-tabs and you can make a tiny theatre inside the box.

You will need
shoe box
tissue paper
stiff paper
ruler and scissors
needle and thread
glue and paints

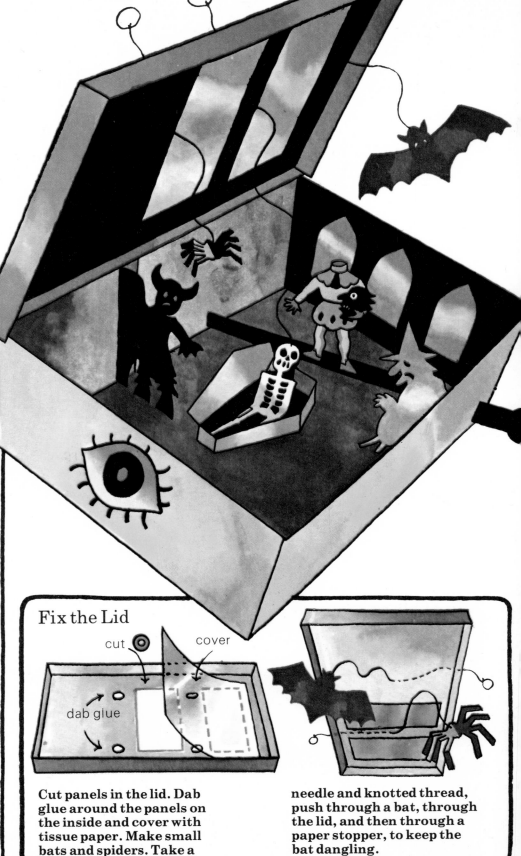

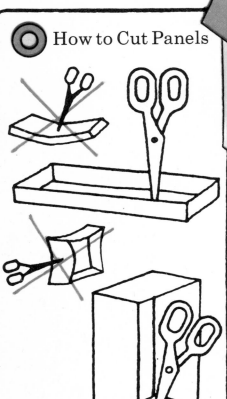

◎ How to Cut Panels

To start, turn the box so that the side you want to cut lies flat against something hard. Jab with the tip of the scissors. Pick it up again to finish.

Fix the Lid

cut ◎

cover

dab glue

Cut panels in the lid. Dab glue around the panels on the inside and cover with tissue paper. Make small bats and spiders. Take a

needle and knotted thread, push through a bat, through the lid, and then through a paper stopper, to keep the bat dangling.

12

1 Fix the Box

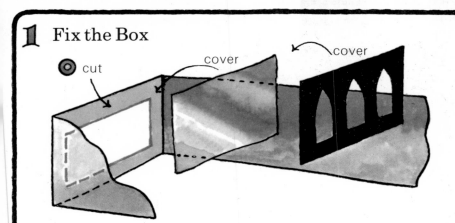

Cut a panel from the back of the box. Turn it into a special window by covering first with tissue paper, then with cut-out paper. Now paint walls and floor.

2

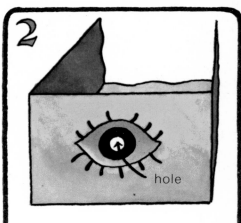

Make a small hole in the front and paint a scarey eye around it.

3

Make stand-out figures and scenery with tabs on one side. Glue tabs to the side of the box. Make figures with tabs at the base to stand up in the middle of the box. They must all face forwards, tabs towards the back.

Action Figure – Prowling Monster

Cut slots in the box and make a long slide of stiff paper. Glue the figure to it. Glue paper stops at the ends. Push back and forth.

Action Figure – Rising Spirit

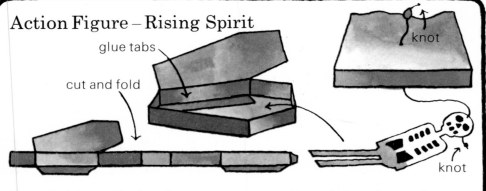

To make the coffin, bend a strip of paper and stick down with tabs. Glue together at the ends. Then make a ghostly figure. Use needle and thread to make a cord that goes through the lid as shown. Pull and the spirit rises – let go and the spirit drops.

Party Crowns and Lanterns

You will need
stiff coloured paper
coloured cellophane
scissors and ruler
sticky tape and glue

You can make the crowns from plain-coloured wrapping paper, but they won't be very strong. Decorate them with cut-out shapes of kitchen foil or silver paper.

Remember – How to Score, p.5 and How to Mark a Straight Line, p.8.

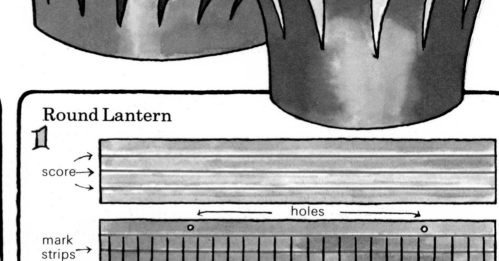

King's Crow

glue shapes

Measure a strip long enough to fit your head, with a bit extra. Score and cut as for a lantern. Then cut designs and glue jewel shapes of paper on the top edge.

glue strip

cut

Tape to fit your head. Glue a strip of stiff paper round the bottom to make it strong. Then cut off a strip as shown and throw it away.

Round Lantern

1

score→

mark strips→

holes

Draw three lines on a long rectangle of paper and score as shown. Then draw even strips in the middle

and decorate them. Make two holes at the top, about half-way from the centre.

2

fold

roll and glue

cut

knot string

Fold on the middle scored line. Cut out the strips as shown. Open up, roll into a

tube and glue. Thread and tie string to hang.

14

Squares and Rectangles

A rectangle is a shape with four sides and four square corners. A square is a special kind of rectangle. All four sides of a square are the same length.

1 Shadow Lantern

← 50 cm →

12½ cm

stick down cellophane

— cut
— score

Cut out a strip of four squares with tabs as shown and an extra square. Inside each square mark a border and draw a shape attached

to the border at several points. Cut out bits around the shape. Glue cellophane over the cut-outs and score round the squares.

Queen's Crown

cut from the fold

Measure a strip long enough to fit around your head. Cut out jewel shapes around the top and cover at the back with cellophane. Then make a strip of lacy paper. Fold as for paper cut-outs. Make fancy shapes by cutting from the fold. Unfold. Glue to the edge of the crown. Roll and tape to fit your head.

2

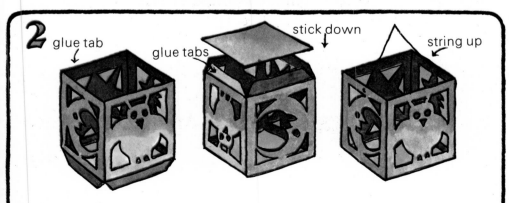

glue tab

glue tabs

stick down

string up

Now bend into a box and glue together with the side tab. Turn upside-down to put glue on the bottom tabs and press

down the extra square. Now make holes in opposite corners at the top to tie a string through.

Mobiles

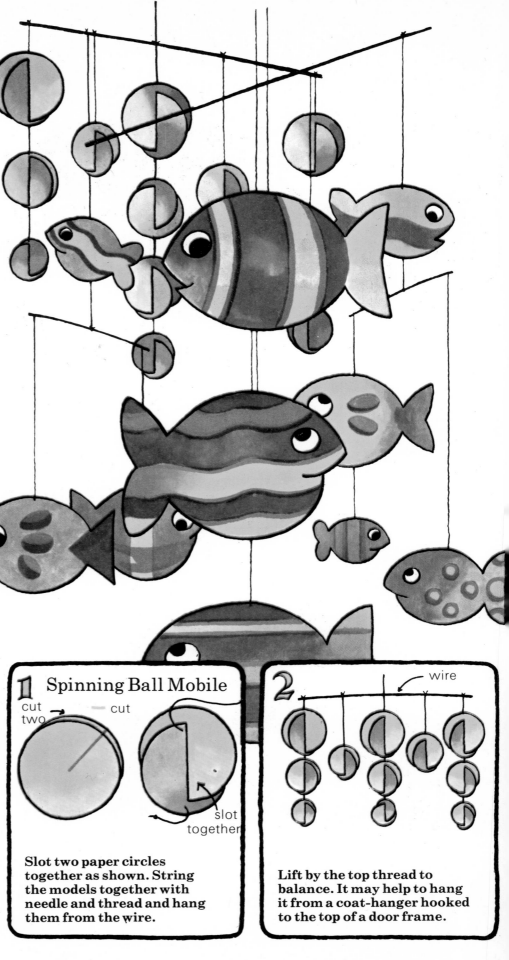

Blow on the mobile very gently to make it move. The balance is so delicate that it will move with currents of air that you don't even notice. Each hanging piece has a balance point and the arms of each move from side to side as well as up and down. Once you see how the balance works, you can invent new moving patterns.

You will need
wire or thin sticks
button thread (strong thread)
stiff paper and glue
scissors and needle

Balancing a Mobile

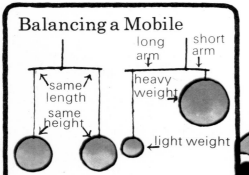

If both arms of a mobile are the same length, they balance equal weights. A short arm balances a heavier weight against a long arm.

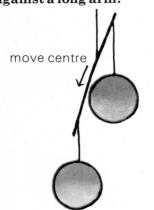

When a mobile doesn't balance, move the centre thread very gradually towards the down end. Do this for each hanging piece.

1 Spinning Ball Mobile

Slot two paper circles together as shown. String the models together with needle and thread and hang them from the wire.

2

Lift by the top thread to balance. It may help to hang it from a coat-hanger hooked to the top of a door frame.

16

Lacy Lanterns

Folded paper is hard to cut through, so use the thinnest paper you can find. Make the cuts very deep and as close together as possible. When you first make the lantern it will be shaped like a flying saucer. As it hangs, it will gradually open up.

You will need
thin paper and scissors
string and glue
stiff paper for the base and top

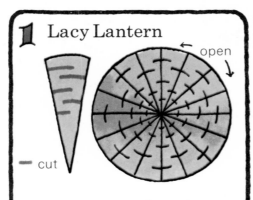

1 Lacy Lantern

open

cut

Cut two paper circles, using a big plate. Fold each in half four times. Then make very deep cuts from the sides as shown. Open flat.

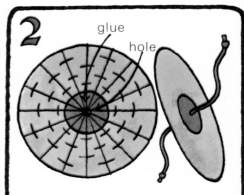

2 glue
hole

Glue small circles of stiff paper to the centre of each. When dry, make a hole in one of these and thread with string. Knot both ends.

Flying Fish Mobile

This pattern uses three balancing pieces. Make all the models first and lay the whole pattern flat on a table to fit together.

3 spot glue

press down

Turn the other circle. Spot glue on every other fold. Press the threaded circle on the sticky circle. When dry, pull carefully apart.

Paper Soldiers

You will need
stiff paper
ruler and scissors
pencil and paints
glue

Remember – use strong glue with a nozzle, so that you can dab spots of glue to add cut-out eyes, moustache, etc. Use a pencil end when your fingertips get sticky.

1 Paper Soldier

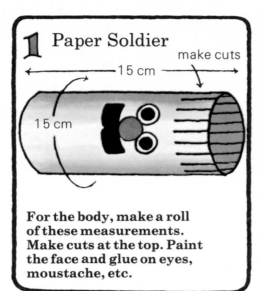

make cuts

15 cm

15 cm

For the body, make a roll of these measurements. Make cuts at the top. Paint the face and glue on eyes, moustache, etc.

2

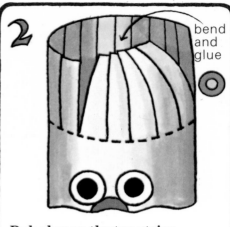

bend and glue

Dab glue on the top strips. Bend one on top of another to make a dome shape.

How to Curl

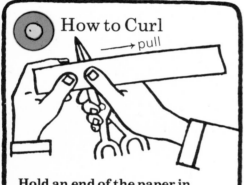

→ pull

Hold an end of the paper in one hand. With the other, hold it tightly between thumb and closed scissors and pull away with a quick, sharp movement.

5

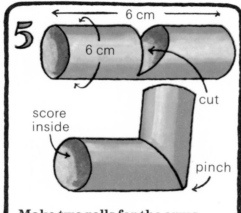

6 cm

6 cm

cut

score inside

pinch

Make two rolls for the arms and glue one to the body. Cut the other as shown. Score it at the bend.

6

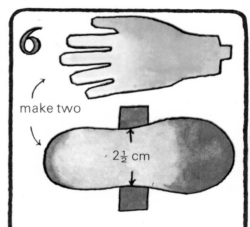

make two

2½ cm

Make hands and feet with tabs, from these patterns. Curl the hands.

Gluing Paper Sculpture

press with pencil

To glue a roll, press the join with a pencil held inside as shown. Use a pencil whenever you can't reach inside.

8

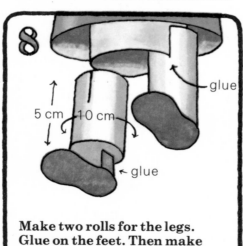

glue

5 cm   10 cm

glue

Make two rolls for the legs. Glue on the feet. Then make cuts as shown to slot the legs to the body.

9

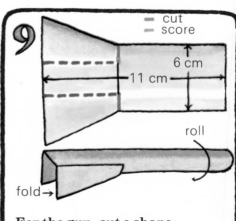

cut
score

6 cm

11 cm

roll

fold →

For the gun, cut a shape with these measurements. Cut and score. Then fold and roll as shown.

3 mark and draw · cut

Hold a piece of paper around the body to make a cone shape and draw the jacket as shown. Then cut out the jacket.

4 score

Cut and score the jacket neck as shown. Bend at the scored line to glue to the body. Join at back. Glue on a collar.

push down · curl

For the hat, glue a long strip of curled fringe round the head. Push down an extra bit of fringe.

7 glue

Glue the bending elbow to the body and glue both hands to the arms.

Paper People

KnowHow Circle-Maker

3 cm 6 cm 9 cm

Measure and punch holes in a strip of cardboard. Stick pencils through two holes. Hold one pencil firm and swing the other around.

Hats with Brims

cut
score

fold out

pinch

roll sides

Trace around the head and score this mark. Then draw a larger circle and cut it out. Make cuts from the centre to the scored line.

Push the head through the centre. Glue a strip around the top. Pinch front or roll sides to make different brims.

Faces

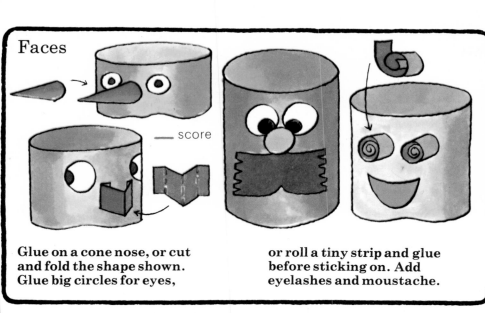

Glue on a cone nose, or cut and fold the shape shown. Glue big circles for eyes,

or roll a tiny strip and glue before sticking on. Add eyelashes and moustache.

Hair

cover —

— score
bald head

Cut and score a strip of paper as shown. Curl the bottom strips. Bend and glue

the top strips to the head. Cover with a circle, or stick paper curls all over.

Cone Hats

5 cm

2 cm

Make a semi-circle at least 2½ times as big across as the head. Use the KnowHow Circle-Maker. Roll into a cone and glue.

— cut

cotton wool

For a Santa Claus hat, glue on cotton wool. For a Robin Hood hat, slice off the top. Make cuts in a feather shape and glue it on.

For finger puppets, make tubes that fit your fingers.

Paperville

Make a small house first, to see how the pattern works. It's easy to make if you start at the edge of the paper and first measure all the lines across, then the lines going down. Remember – How to Mark a Straight Line, p.7.

You will need
large sheets of stiff paper
scissors, ruler
pencil, glue and paints

Chimney

1

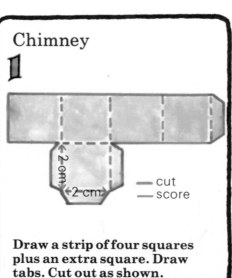

2 cm.
2 cm.

— cut
— score

Draw a strip of four squares plus an extra square. Draw tabs. Cut out as shown.

2

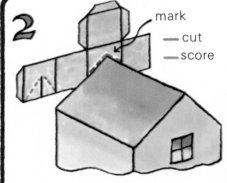

mark
— cut
— score

Hold next to the roof and mark the shape on every other square. Cut and score both as shown and fold in the triangles.

House

1

measure in cm

throw away

← 7 →←← 6 →←← 7 →|

3
6
6
6
3

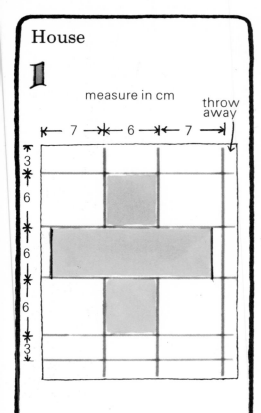

Measure three lines from the side of the paper, like the red lines. Then start from the top and measure down to make five lines, like the blue lines.

2

cut
score

centre   throw away

base

1 cm tab

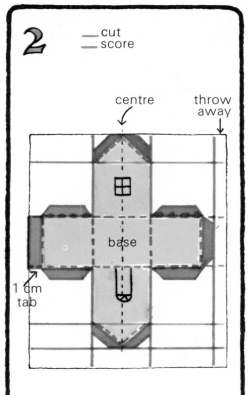

Draw lines from a centre point to the sides as shown. Draw tabs. Make doors and windows. Then score all round the base and along the tabs. Cut out.

3

← 6 cm →

9 cm

Fold the tabs, fold up the house and glue. For a roof that just fits, fold paper measured as shown. Make it bigger to stick out.

3

Dab glue on the roof and fold the chimney round, using the folded triangles as tabs. Glue into a box.

4

cut
score

For a chimney pot, make a small tube. Cut and score one end to bend inwards and glue it to the chimney.

Making Boxes

base

equal
equal
equal

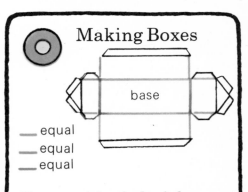

You can make the basic box-shape as long or as tall as you like. But remember –
1. Make all the sides equal.
2. Make opposite sides of the base equal.

Paperville Street

Road Signs

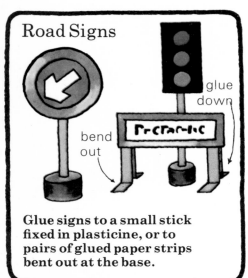

Glue signs to a small stick fixed in plasticine, or to pairs of glued paper strips bent out at the base.

bend out

glue down

Trees

slot

cut

Make two tree-top shapes. Cut to the centre of each and slot together. Make a roll for the trunk. When dry, **make four cuts in the top, spaced to slot in the tree-top. Make cuts in the base and bend out. Glue in place.**

bend out

paper fringe

fold-up porch

stick-on slates

fold-out awning

cut
score

open

push to open

box

fruit tab

Cut and score the doors and shutters before gluing the house together. Stick on extra pieces afterwards.

Paperville Church

Church Steeple

cut

score

same width

Make a long house for the church. Measure the end and mark that width four times on paper – or five or six times, for a steeple with more sides. Draw the steeple sides and tabs and score as shown. Colour the steeple and make the doors and windows. Cut it out, glue the tabs and glue it on.

Paperville Railway

Paperville Express

Join the matchbox trays with needle and knotted thread. For the engine, fit two trays together and glue a box in front. For the boiler, make cuts in the end of a tube. Bend in and glue on. Add a funnel to let out the steam (cotton wool). Fold paper to go around the cab and cut out the sides as shown. Don't forget the dials and brake. Stick toothpicks through cardboard wheels (cut round a button) and tape.

cut
score
fold
tape
rolled-paper brake

You will find tips on making the station-house and awning on pages 22 to 25.

Tape strips of stiff paper to heavy string. Then you can curve the track to go where you like.

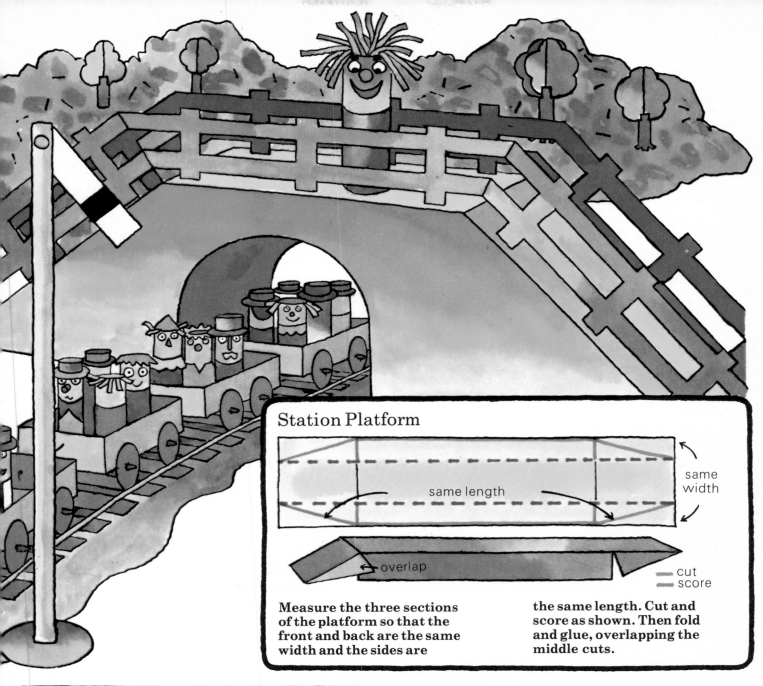

Station Platform

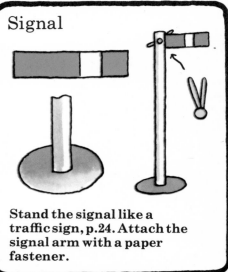

same width

same length

overlap

cut
score

Measure the three sections of the platform so that the front and back are the same width and the sides are the same length. Cut and score as shown. Then fold and glue, overlapping the middle cuts.

Bridge

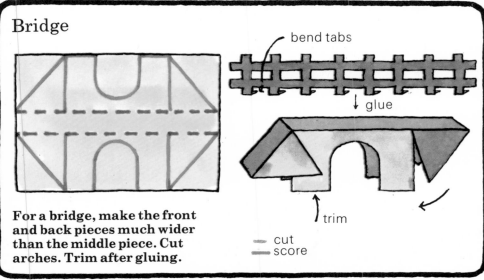

bend tabs

↓ glue

trim

cut
score

For a bridge, make the front and back pieces much wider than the middle piece. Cut arches. Trim after gluing.

Signal

Stand the signal like a traffic sign, p.24. Attach the signal arm with a paper fastener.

Papier Mâché Landscape

Papier mâché is made of layers of newspaper soaked in paste. When it is wet it can be modelled and it becomes very hard when dry. The smaller the pieces of newspaper, the stronger the papier mâché will be.

You will need
strong cardboard for the base
large bowl or basin for mixing
newspaper and cold-water paste
poster paint and glue
stiff paper and scissors
mirror or kitchen foil

Make papier mâché by soaking pieces of newspaper in a bowl of cold-water paste. Then build up slopes and hills on a cardboard base. While the landscape is drying, weight the edges or tack them down to an old board to keep them from curling. Drying time is two to three days. When dry, paint with poster paints.

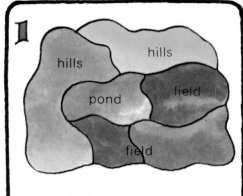

Mark the base in sections of hills, fields and pond. Don't cover this line with papier mâché or it will be too hard to cut when dry.

28

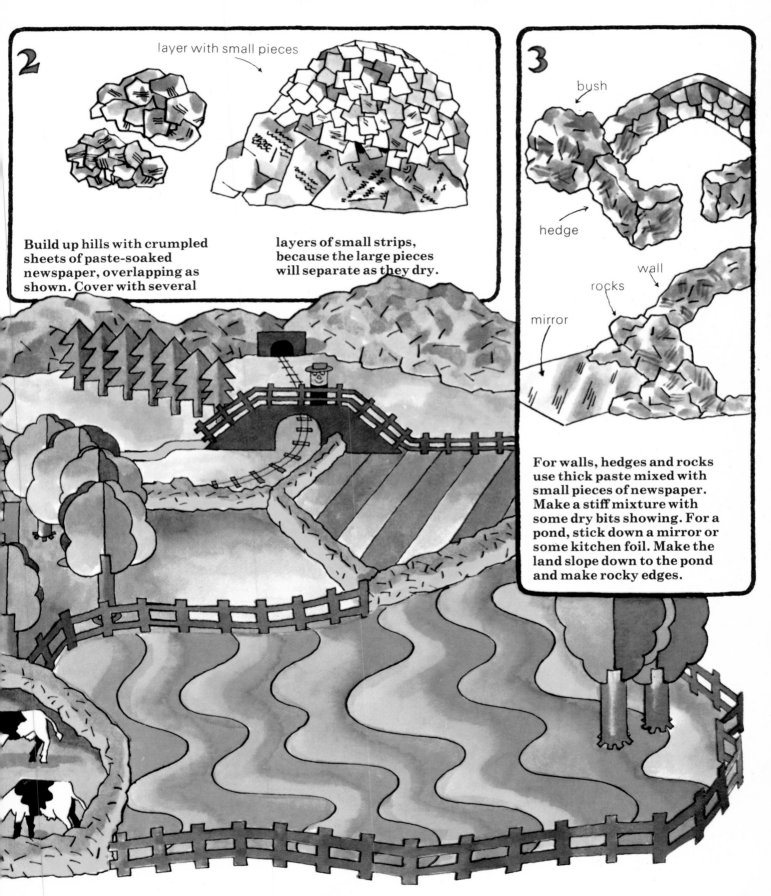

2

layer with small pieces

Build up hills with crumpled sheets of paste-soaked newspaper, overlapping as shown. Cover with several layers of small strips, because the large pieces will separate as they dry.

3

bush

hedge

rocks

wall

mirror

For walls, hedges and rocks use thick paste mixed with small pieces of newspaper. Make a stiff mixture with some dry bits showing. For a pond, stick down a mirror or some kitchen foil. Make the land slope down to the pond and make rocky edges.

Paper Zoo

To make a stand-up animal, just cut the shape with its back along a fold. Then you can curl, glue and fold to make bending necks, curling tails and 3-D ears and wings. You will find patterns for all the animals on the next pages.

You will need
stiff paper
scissors and glue
paints or crayons to decorate
Remember – How to Score, p.5. and How to Curl, p.18.

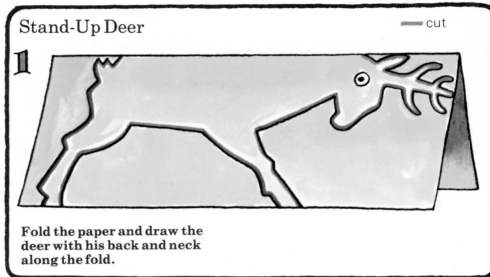

Stand-Up Deer

— cut

1

Fold the paper and draw the deer with his back and neck along the fold.

3   fold back

Fold back the head and neck and crease.

4

push down

push back.

Push the fold down and push the neck back as shown.

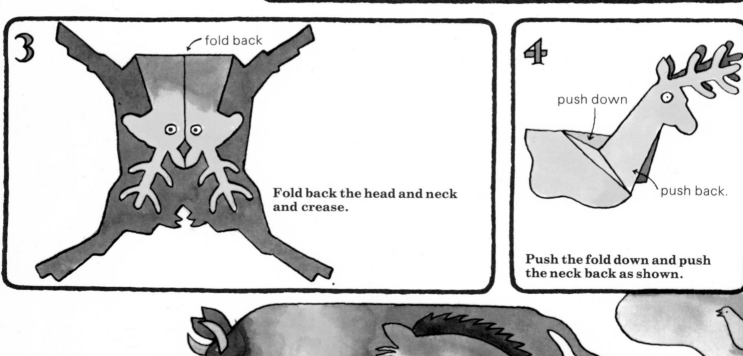

2

— score

Open flat and score as shown.

Paper Zoo Patterns

Piglet

curl

cut two

Cut ear shapes with a tab. Curl the ears and tail before gluing them on.

Mouse

push down

fold back

— score

Fold and score as shown. Push down and back so that the mouse's head is tucked

between its shoulders. Add a long curling tail. Hang by the tail.

Lion and Tiger

curl

cut two

For the lion's mane, cut a deep fringe in a strip of

paper. Curl the fringe. Fold and glue on the neck.

Flapping Duck

— score

Score and fold the wing and glue it to the duck. If the duck is nose-heavy, put a very tiny bit of plasticine behind its tail.

Seal

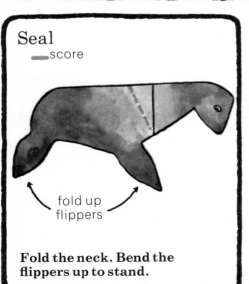

— score

fold up flippers

Fold the neck. Bend the flippers up to stand.

Snake

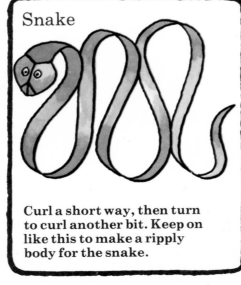

Curl a short way, then turn to curl another bit. Keep on like this to make a ripply body for the snake.

Giraffe

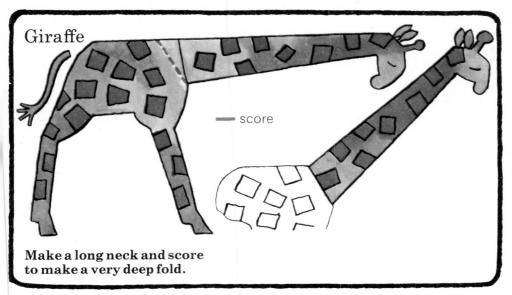

— score

Make a long neck and score to make a very deep fold.

Duck and Chicken

— score

Fold over a wing shape, fringed as shown.

Cow and Elephant

cut two

curl

Curl tusks before gluing on.

Pony

— cut
— score

glue mane

Make a neck fold as for the deer. Then slit along the neck and glue a fringed mane between the neck halves.

Add a tail the same way. To lower the head, just push down the neck and crease again.

Zebra

— cut
— score

The zebra is like the pony.

C•—PF

Castles and Things (1)

You will need

a large cardboard box
stiff paper
straws
glue and sticky tape
a paper fastener
silver foil
a cereal packet
a small pencil
a small strong cardboard box
cardboard
scissors
felt pens and paints

About Castles

On the right is a bird's eye view of the castle above. A soldier enters over the drawbridge and past the outer gatehouse or barbican. The land between the curtain wall and the keep is called the bailey. All the windows in the keep are very narrow. This makes it more difficult for an enemy's arrow to shoot in. On the next three pages you will find out how to make the keep and some of the things that go with it.

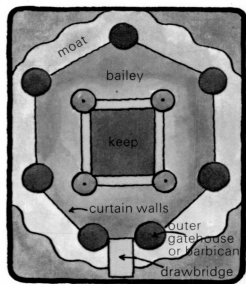

moat

bailey

keep

curtain walls

outer gatehouse or barbican

drawbridge

Battlements

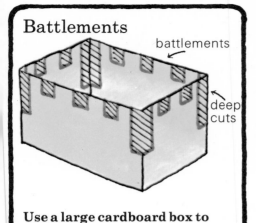

Use a large cardboard box to make a keep. Cut battlements along the top. At each corner make a deeper cut.

1 To Make a Turret

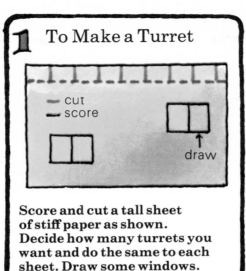

— cut
— score
draw

Score and cut a tall sheet of stiff paper as shown. Decide how many turrets you want and do the same to each sheet. Draw some windows.

2

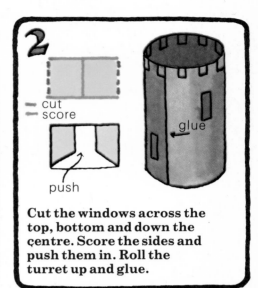

— cut
— score
glue
push

Cut the windows across the top, bottom and down the centre. Score the sides and push them in. Roll the turret up and glue.

3

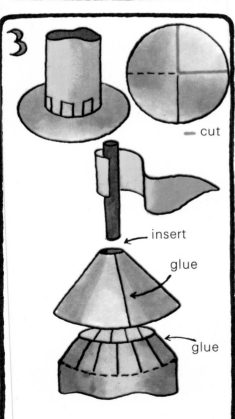

— cut
insert
glue
glue

Cut a circle twice as wide as the tower and cut a piece out of it. Glue the rest into a cone. Glue a paper flag to a straw, snip off the top of the cone and push the straw in. Bend the cuts on the turret top inwards, dab on some glue and press the cone onto the turret.

Finishing the Keep

mark — — mark
slot over

Hold a turret over a corner battlement and make two marks where it touches the keep. Cut two long slots from the two marks on the turret and push the turret onto the corner.

Curtain Walls

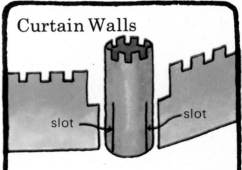

slot — slot

Cut battlements along the top of stiff paper with deeper cuts at each end. Cut two slots in each turret as shown and push the walls in. Make a line of walls.

1,500 Miles of Battlements

The Great Wall of China is so long that it is the only man-made building that can be seen from outer space.

Castles and Things (2)

The Drawbridge

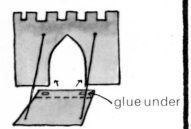

Cut a door out of the wall. Glue card under the door, bend it up against the wall and make two holes above the door as shown. Thread string through the holes and knot.

1 The Rampart Walk

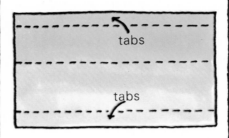

Cut out a piece of stiff paper the same length as the keep wall. Score it as shown. The outer folds are the tabs.

2

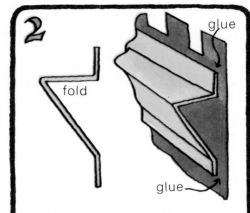

Fold the paper like this. Glue the tabs to the keep just under the battlements. This is a rampart walk.

1 The Siege Tower

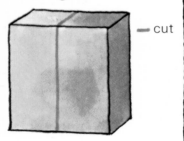

Siege towers are pushed up to the castle walls. The top door opens and out come the soldiers. First cut a cereal packet as shown.

2 For the Floors

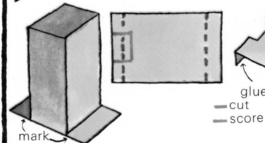

Cut out a piece of stiff paper wider than the box. Put the box on top and draw lines at both sides. Score and cut as shown.

Fold over the tabs and glue them into the box. Draw a ladder running up the inside. Make as many floors as you think it needs.

3 For the Door

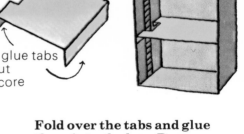

Cut a door opening at the top of the tower. Use a paper fastener as a catch.

4 For the Wheels

Cut out two cardboard circles. Make holes in the centres. Tape a round pencil under the front end of the tower. Slot the wheels on. Crunch silver foil over the pencil ends.

5 Handles and Legs

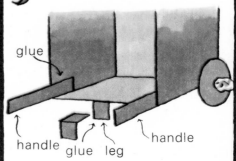

Cut out two card handles and a card leg. Glue them onto the tower.

1 Making a Catapult

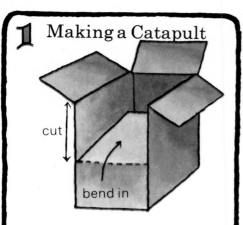

Cut half way down one side of a small strong cardboard box. Bend the flap inwards.

2

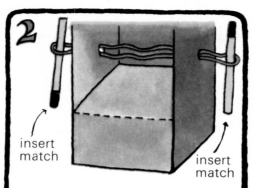

insert match

insert match

Make two holes with your scissors 2½ cm above the flap. Push the ends of a strong rubber band through the holes. Keep the band in there with matches.

3

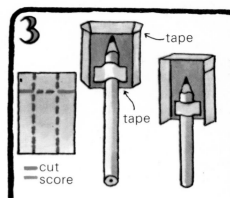

tape

tape

cut
score

Score and cut a small piece of card as shown. Tape the sides up and tape it to the end of a small pencil.

Push the catapult arm back. Put your ammunition in the ammunition holder, let the catapult arm go and fire.

4

Twist the rubber band round and round until you can't twist it any more. Push the catapult arm into its middle.

5

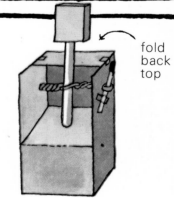

fold back top

Let the catapult arm spring up until it is pointing straight up. Fold back the top front flap and tape.

Whatsits

You will need
thin paper or tissue paper
needle and thread
scissors and pencil
strong glue with a nozzle
stiff paper for decorations
wire and tape for flowers

Remember – don't let spots of glue drip onto the paper. Dab a tiny damp spot from the end of the nozzle and pull the nozzle quickly away. Remember – Know How Circle-Maker, p.20

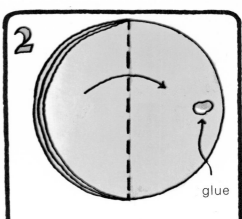

Making a Whatsit

1

Cut ten circles of paper about 8 cm across. Stack neatly and sew through the middle. Fold on the stitch.

2

glue

Fold back one half-circle. Put a dot of glue on the three o'clock spot. Press the next half-circle down.

3

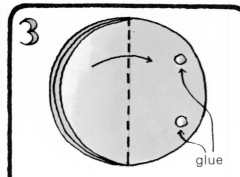

Now dab glue on the two and four o'clock spots and press down another half-circle. Alternate one dot and two dots until all the half-circles are glued down.

4

open

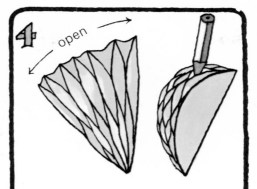

When quite dry, open out the Whatsit. Pull gently apart between the glue spots. For stiff paper, use a pencil to open the spaces.

5

Press between the spaces to glue one side of the base to a circle of stiff paper. When dry, glue the other side down.

Mouse

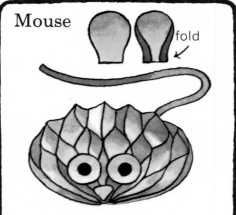

fold

Fold the ears and glue them inside the spaces. Stick on eyes, nose and string tail.

Rabbit

glue

For a rabbit, add a small round tail.

Ladybird

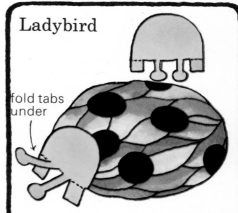

fold tabs under

Cut the shape shown and glue the tabs under the base. Stick on lots of spots.

Flower

Tape some wire to a circle of card and glue between two Whatsits. Cut a long leaf. Wind and glue around the wire.

Pop-Up Card

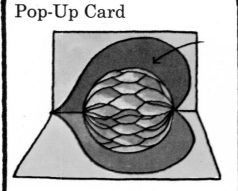

Fold the card. Glue a Whatsit inside with the stitch line right along the fold.

Decorations

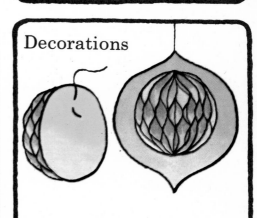

Thread a Whatsit with string. Glue it to a paper shape as shown, or stick two Whatsits together to make a ball.

Paper Flowers

The stretchiness of crêpe paper is very useful. You can pull it into petal shapes or ruffled edges. With tissue paper you can show the vein of a leaf by making a lengthwise crease.

You will need
crêpe paper
tissue paper
sticky tape and scissors
strong glue with a nozzle
thin sticks or light wire (such as florist's wire or medium fuse wire) for the stems

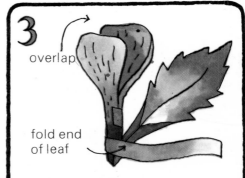

Daisies

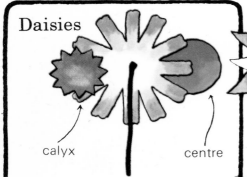

calyx

centre

Cut petals round a circle. Sandwich petals and stem between a centre circle and calyx shape and glue together.

Crêpe Paper Poppies

1

cut a fringe

wind

For the centre, make cuts in a strip of paper as shown. Fasten it to the stem with thread, or glue the edge and wind it round and round.

2

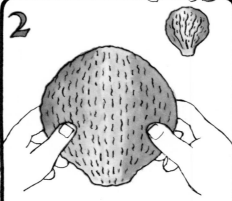

Make eight petals. Cut them with the grain of the paper running up and down. Shape them by stretching sideways.

3

overlap

fold end of leaf

Glue the petals one by one around the stem. Then glue a long strip of paper under the flower and wind it down the stem, gluing in leaf shapes as you do so.

Tissue Paper Roses

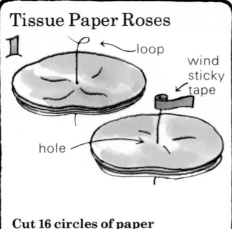

1 loop — wind sticky tape — hole

Cut 16 circles of paper about 16 cm across. Make a wire stem as shown.

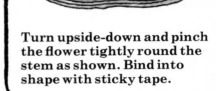

2

Turn upside-down and pinch the flower tightly round the stem as shown. Bind into shape with sticky tape.

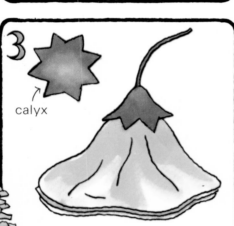

3 calyx

Cut out a calyx. Slide it down the stem and glue it to the flower.

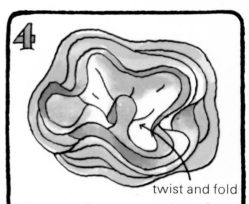

4 twist and fold

Turn the flower up again and shape it by pulling the petals out as shown. Twist and fold to make a centre. Cover the stem as before.

Carnations

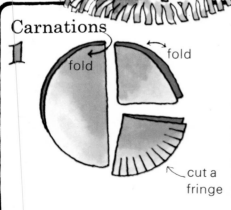

1 fold — fold — cut a fringe

Cut 13 circles of thin paper, about 9 cm across. Fold each into a quarter-circle. Make cuts as shown.

2 glue

Open one circle flat. Glue the quarter-circles onto it in layers as shown.

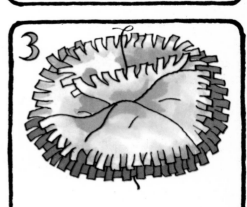

3

Loop the end of some wire and push it through to make a stem. Glue a strip of green paper round the stem.

Crocodile Marionette

Paper Spring

1

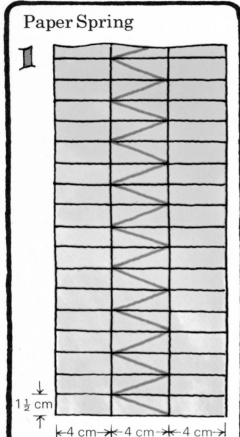

↕ 1½ cm

|← 4 cm →|← 4 cm →|← 4 cm →|

Use paper 12 cm wide and as long as possible. If you glue strips together, let the glue dry before you do the next step. Rule lines as shown and make a coloured zig-zag down the centre.

The body of this crocodile marionette is made from a strip of paper folded into a special spring. This makes a shape that can bend and twist and wriggle when you move the hanging strings. The fold is tricky until you get the knack, so follow the instructions carefully.

Remember – How to Mark a Straight Line, p.8.

You will need
coloured paper
ruler and scissors
glue and string
coloured pencil or felt pen
2 small sticks or rods

Turn the page to see how to make the head of the crocodile and how to work the strings.

2

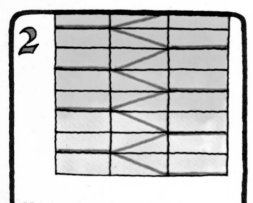

Now make coloured lines joining the points of the zig-zag to the edges. Score all the coloured lines and crease them firmly.

3

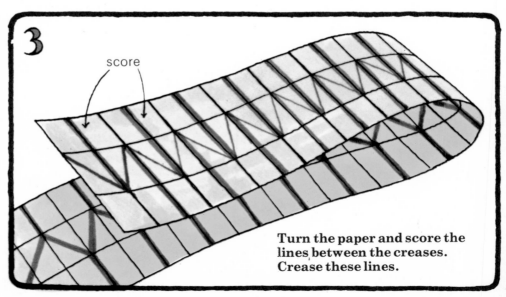

score

Turn the paper and score the lines between the creases. Crease these lines.

4 Hold the paper as shown. Walk your thumbs along the sides to push the creases inwards and pinch the folds between your fingers.

5 Continue until all the folds can be pinched between your fingers to make a shape like this.

Crocodile Marionette (2)

Make the Croc

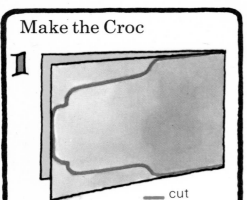

1 Take some paper about 40 cm long and 10 cm wide and fold in half. Draw and cut out the head shape.

cut

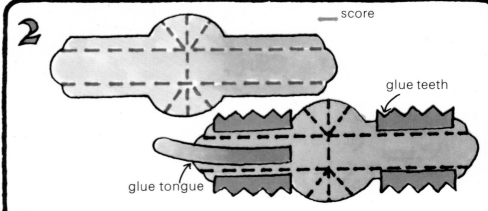

score

glue teeth

glue tongue

2 Open and score as shown. Turn the head and glue strips of paper teeth inside the jaw.

Glue the end of a long tongue to the back of the top jaw.

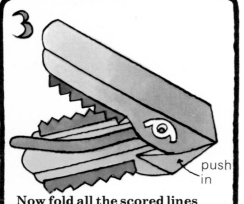

push in

3 Now fold all the scored lines inward. Push in the crease between the V-shaped score at each side of the jaw.

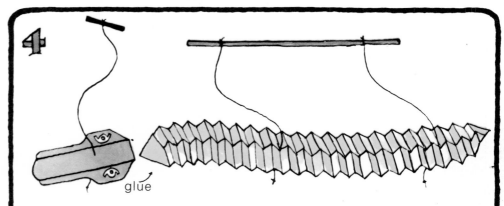

glue

4 Glue the paper spring to the back of the head. String up the crocodile with a needle and knotted thread as shown.

Tie the head string to a small stick. Tie the two back strings to another stick.

Work the Croc

Raise the head string to make the crocodile rear up and jerk the string to make its jaws open and close.

Rock the stick back and forth to make the crocodile hump its back as it moves along.

Hold your arms like this to make the crocodile turn and chase its tail.

Jack-in-the-Box

You will need
thin card for the box
coloured paper
ruler and pencil
scissors and glue

As you open the box, give it a
shake to make the Jack jump out.
If the Jack loses its spring
after a while, stretch it out and
fold it up again.
Remember – Making Boxes, p.23.

1

glue

**Make a paper spring 10 cm
wide and as long as possible.
Glue it to a head made from
a paper circle 10 cm across.**

2

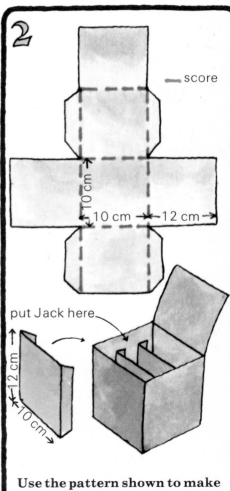

score

10 cm

10 cm → ← 12 cm

put Jack here

12 cm

10 cm

**Use the pattern shown to make
a box. Glue pieces with tabs
inside the box to hold the
Jack upright.**

3

folded strip

paper slide

slotted strip

**Fold a strip of paper and
glue it to the lid as shown.
Cut another strip with a
stand-up slot and glue it
to the front. Lock the box
with a slide of stiff paper.**

Tips on What to Use

Here are some suggestions to help you find the right materials for the projects.

Acetate – Look for acetate tops on boxes of greeting cards, handkerchiefs or perfume. You can buy rolls of acetate at an art supply shop, but it's very expensive to buy this way.

Canes and florists' wire – Buy at a gardening shop or at a florist's.

Cellophane – Buy it in small rolls at an art supply shop. It doesn't cost much.

Cold-water paste – Buy Rex Cold-water Paste at an art supply shop or buy wallpaper paste at a hardware shop. Wallpaper paste is not a good thing to get in your mouth, so be sure to wash your hands when you have used it.

Glue – Use strong glue with a nozzle, like Bostik 1 or UHU.

Fuse wire – Buy at Woolworth's.

Medium galvanized wire – Buy at Woolworth's.

Sticky tape – Use Scotch Tape, if you can find it. It's very strong and doesn't split.

Stiff coloured paper – You can buy it in sheets at an art supply shop. Ask for cartridge paper. It can be light or heavy, so be sure to say what you want it for.

Thin paper – Buy at an art supply shop. Ask for a layout pad or for sheets of detail paper.

Cartridge paper and detail paper are sold in packets at many stationery shops, but the sheets are too small for several of the projects.

Did You Know?

You can buy paper that is strong enough to bear the weight of a car.

Did you Know?

Up to 20 miles of paper can be produced every hour by a large papermaking machine.